A Mother's

First-Year Journal

DIMENSIONS
FOR LIVING

NASHVILLE

A MOTHER'S FIRST-YEAR JOURNAL

First Month

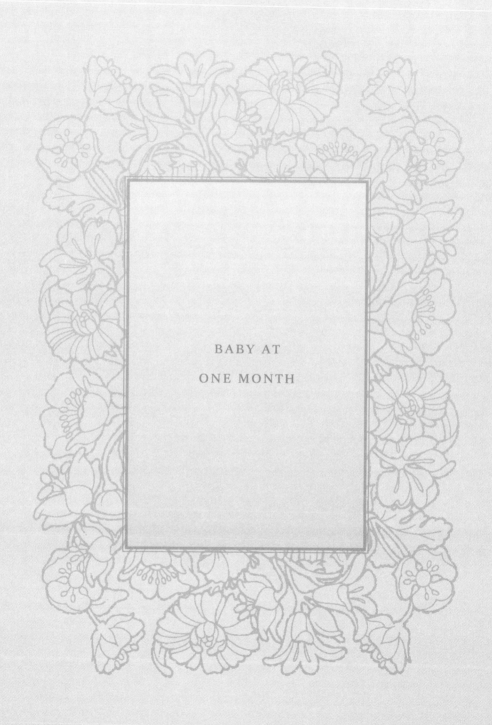

BABY AT

ONE MONTH

We spend many hours preparing for childbirth. We review the relaxation and breathing techniques. We re-read books on pregnancy and childbirth. We lovingly prepare the nursery. Although we cannot predict the exact day or hour that our baby will arrive, we wait with joyous anticipation, for we know htat we are well prepared.

In spite of all our preparations, labor often doesn't proceed as we expect, and the thought of experiencing hours of such intense pain is frightening. Then the unbearable pain we experienced just moments ago is almost forgotten as feelings of indescribable joy come over us when we hold our tiny miracle for the first time.

Those of us who have given birth may be able to understand more fully Jesus' teachings about the kingdom of heaven. We have prepared ourselves well, yet the actual event of childbirth comes as a surprise and goes beyond our wildest expectations. We have experienced pain, but the joy of giving birth far surpasses the intensity of that pain.

Isn't that part of what the kingdom of heaven is about? Although Jesus did not use the image of childbirth in his teachings about the kingdom of heaven, he did teach that those who are prepared for the Kingdom can wait in eager anticipation, knowing that although there may be pain along the way, they will experience surprise beyond belief, joy beyond expectation, and life beyond life.

Almighty God, thank you for the miracle of life.

—*Helen Hempfling Enari*

My Thoughts & Feelings

We can honor God by joining in the amazement of new life with joy.

My Prayer Journey

You created my inner being and formed me in my mother's womb. I will praise you because I am fearfully and wonderfully made. —Psalm 139:13-14

Baby's Growth & Development

Weight _____

Length _____

New Skills _____

_____

_____

Observations:

Memorable Moments

Second Month

BABY AT

TWO MONTHS

Any new mother, living in a state of perpetual exhaustion, would be comforted by the words of Isaiah 40:31: "Those who wait for the LORD *shall renew their strength, they shall mount up with wings like eagles, they shall run and not be weary, they shall walk and not faint" (NRSV). The problem is the word* wait. *We may feel like asking God why we have to wait so much! Why can't we have instantaneous strenth, vigor, and energy?*

A new mother's prayer often is "Lord, give me patience RIGHT NOW!" Having to wait makes us realize that any semblance of patience or strengh we have is sheer gift. We are not in control; we cannot summon these gifts by an act of will.

It is that very powerlessness that makes motherhood so difficult and so life-changing. We are forced to rely on God to get through each day. As we shed the illusion of being in control, we become healthier human beings.

Lord, help me to wait on you, trusting in that day when I will run without fainting from exhaustion.

—Joan Laney

My Thoughts & Feelings

God's love gives mothers the strength, patience, and power to love our children.

My Prayer Journey

As for me and my house, we will serve the Lord. —Joshua 24:15 KJV

Baby's Growth & Development

Weight _____

Length _____

New Skills _____

_____

_____

Observations:

Memorable Moments

Third Month

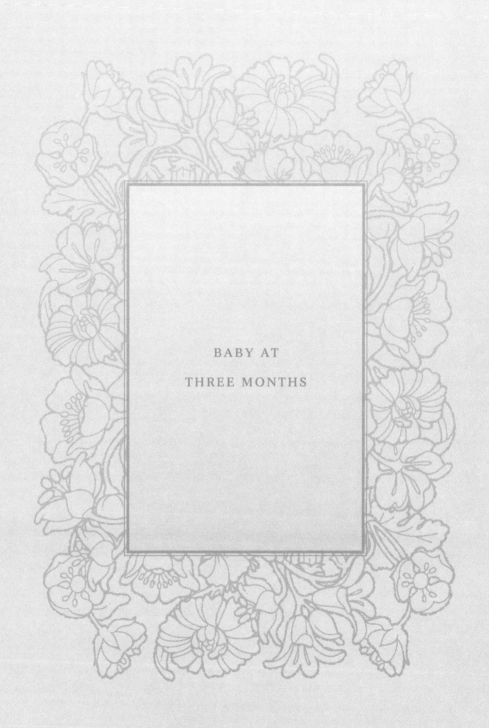

BABY AT

THREE MONTHS

It would be impossible for a nursing mother to forget about her child. If by some miracle an infant were to sleep quietly through a feeding, thus allowing the mother to pay attention to other matters, the heaviness of her full to overflowing breasts would cause enough discomfort to remind her of the child. There is a physical interconnectedness between a nursing mother and her baby.

How marvelous it is to think that there is a similar, undeniable bond between God and us. Isaiah 49:15 promises that it is easier for a nursing mother to forget her child than it is for God to forget us. Every few hours a nursing mother comes close, skin to skin, with her child. Can it be that throughout the day God is as available for intimate, nourishing contact with us if we but cry out and acknowledge our great need for comfort and care?

Thank you, O God, for your loving, constant care.

—Rebecca Laird

My Thoughts & Feelings

Even more faithful than a mother, God never forgets his children.

My Prayer Journey

_____

_____

_____

_____

_____

_____

_____

_____

_____

_____

_____

_____

_____

_____

_____

_____

_____

Can a mother forget her nursing child and feel no compassion for her baby? Even if she were to forget, I will not forget you. —Isaiah 49:15

Baby's Growth & Development

Weight _____

Length _____

New Skills _____

_____

_____

Observations:

Memorable Moments

Fourth Month

BABY AT

FOUR MONTHS

*S*ince you became a mother, have you spent much time thinking of yourself as a child?

  We are the children of God. We are God's own special possessions. We have been given dominion over the earth, and God expects us to be good stewards of what he has given us. God wants us to serve him. God doesn't want our leftovers. God wants our minds, bodies, hearts, and souls. God wants our availability. Sometimes this frightens us. We fear what God might ask of us. We must learn to trust God more—to think of ourselves as children of God.

Help me, O God, to have the faith of a child and to trust in you always.

—Iris R. Jones-Gboizo

My Thoughts & Feelings

Children awaken us to life and this world by their freshness.

My Prayer Journey

Those who do not receive the kingdom of God as a little child will not enter it.

—Mark 10:15

Baby's Growth & Development

Weight _____

Length _____

New Skills _____

_____

_____

Observations:

Memorable Moments

Fifth Month

BABY AT

FIVE MONTHS

What an awesome responsibility mothers have to their children. Cultural stereotypes promote the idea that giving birth miraculously endows a woman with kindness, compassion, and goodness. But we all know better. Many of us can witness that we are made more aware of our weaknesses and impatience after we bring our newborns home from the hospital than we were before. Godliness and generosity are not prerequisites of giving birth; they are characteristics that God hones and whittles into our characters over time. Motherhood provides a rigorous training ground where we can daily practice and model the disciplines of love, honesty, and compassion before our children.

Dear God, help me to teach my child what it means to be a Christian by my daily example.

—Rebecca Laird

My Thoughts & Feelings

Though we lay down our lives for her we can never pay the debt we owe to a Christian mother. —from "My Mother," author unknown

My Prayer Journey

Train children in the right way, and when old, they will not stray.

—Proverbs 22:6 NRSV

Baby's Growth & Development

Weight _____

Length _____

New Skills _____

_____

_____

Observations:

Memorable Moments

Sixth Month

_____

BABY AT

SIX MONTHS

*S*haring the early months and years of our children's lives bonds women as friends for the rest of our lives. There is something about those consultations, often over the phone, about runny noses, temper tantrums, and sleep patterns that builds a kind of special trust. Perhaps sometimes it is simply not-knowing together.

New mothers need good friends. They need the connection, the sense of being part of a web that is the world of other women who understand what it is like to live in the stretch of maintaining a personal identity when most hours are devoted to others.

A primary characteristic of these friendships is mutuality. Much of the time, what we need is not solutions but a listening ear and empathy.

Help me, O God, to be a listening ear and an encouraging friend to another mother.

—Mary Zimmer

My Thoughts & Feelings

Understanding friends help to make the challenges of life and motherhood seem less difficult.

My Prayer Journey

Beloved, let us love one another: for love is of God.   —1 John 4:7 KJV

Baby's Growth & Development

Weight _____

Length _____

New Skills _____

_____

_____

Observations:

Memorable Moments

Seventh Month

BABY AT

SEVEN MONTHS

Every mother can appreciate Psalm 131. So much of motherhood is submitting ourselves to the demands of others, always being on call for the children. So much of motherhood is not being in control when we would so love to be in control. So much of motherhood is tending to trivial matters.

The psalm likens us to a weaned child clinging to its mother. It means that God loves us as unconditionally as we love our children. It means that this all-powerful God holds us as tenderly as we would hold our children. We need that tenderness. We need that love. When we are discouraged, we can imagine God telling us that all will be well, like a mother comforting us.

Dear God, I am grateful for your unconditional love.

—Joan Laney

My Thoughts & Feelings

There is never a moment when God is not aware of the needs of his children.

My Prayer Journey

I have stilled and quieted my soul; like a weaned child with its mother.

—Psalm 131:2 NIV

Baby's Growth & Development

Weight _____

Length _____

New Skills _____

_____

_____

Observations:

Memorable Moments

Eighth Month

BABY AT

EIGHT MONTHS

*W*ith babies, you never quite know what kind of day they are going to have. They are affected by the amount of sleep they had the night before, the new teeth that may be coming in, the emotional state of their moms on that day, and on and on. So, as mothers, we never know quite what type of day we'll have.

On an average day, many things happen that we may not expect: a spilled cup of something, a temper tantrum, unexplained crying, a soiled crib sheet—the usual daily messes! By the end of the day, most new mothers are worn out and feeling rather frazzled.

But then bedtime comes, the children are tucked in, and they are quiet and so peaceful. We stand there, tired and frazzled, but we think how good it is. We have an idea of how God felt after creating the world—the same way we feel after tucking our children in bed. It is good, very good.

O God, thank you for this family of mine. It is good; it is very good!

—*Leanne H. Ciampa*

My Thoughts & Feelings

Children teach us so much about God's creation.

My Prayer Journey

Then our sons in their youth will be like well-nutured plants, and our daughters will be like pillars carved to adorn a palace. . . . Blessed are the people whose God is the LORD. —Psalm 144:12, 15 NIV

Baby's Growth & Development

Weight _____

Length _____

New Skills _____

_____

_____

Observations:

Memorable Moments

Ninth Month

BABY AT

NINE MONTHS

*S*ometimes a mother looks at her children and thinks, "What would you do without me?" She feeds them, bathes them, and gives them shelter and security. Even as they grow and become more independent, they are still babies needing their mother's love. And they never question that love. They know that if they need food, Mother will get it for them; or if they need a blanket on a cold night, Mother will get it for them. There is no need that, if she is able, she will not provide for them.

That is what Jesus was talking about when he promised to always care for us. He promised to go prepare a place for us and return to take us there. And we, like children depending on our mothers, can depend on his words. For Christ will provide all that we need, not only for this life but also for our life eternal.

Thank you, O God, for providing all the warmth, love, and security we will ever need.

—*Leanne H. Ciampa*

My Thoughts & Feelings

If I should never see another miracle, my mother's love will have been enough.
—George Douglas

My Prayer Journey

Anyone who does not love others does not know God, because God is love.

—1 John 4:8

Baby's Growth & Development

Weight _____

Length _____

New Skills _____

_____

_____

Observations:

Memorable Moments

Tenth Month

BABY AT

TEN MONTHS

No matter how hard we try to shake it, we seem always to be haunted by the tension between what we need to do, can do, and want to do. Often those categories blur. Looking at a situation squarely can be helpful. Looking to God is even better. "I will instruct thee and teach thee in the way which thou shalt go: I will guide thee with mine eye" (Psalm 32:8 KJV). As we learn to look where God is directing, we will be guided. Sometimes this may mean that the laundry has to wait while a diaper is changed, or that there are left-overs for supper because someone is rocked to sleep. If we keep on "making eye contact" with the Instructor, he will enable us to focus our minds and choose what is most important.

God, help me to know what is most important in these precious moments with my young child.

—Kathleen Turner

My Thoughts & Feelings

Each day a mother experiences the newness of her child.

My Prayer Journey

Do not stop the little children from coming to me, for it is to such as these that the kingdom of God belongs. —Luke 18:16

Baby's Growth & Development

Weight _____

Length _____

New Skills _____

_____

_____

Observations:

Memorable Moments

Eleventh Month

BABY AT

ELEVEN MONTHS

*W*atching young children learn to walk is often both amusing and heartrending. They have earned the name toddler because that is what they do. Before children reach that stage, they go through a long apprentice period. This time consists of pulling up, letting go, trying with one foot and then the other, stumbling, falling, whimpering, or just sitting and looking perplexed and then rolling over to start the whole process once again.

The spiritual gift of prayer is a similar reality for most adults. We decide to make prayer a significant part of our daily lives. Perhaps we buy a guide or book of meditations. But on a busy day, our quiet time for prayer, study, and meditation may be the first sacrifice.

A life of prayer is a matter of adopting the toddler's approach to walking. There will be many attempts, some spills and dissatisfaction, and renewed efforts before we come to the stage of determined hunger to be a person of prayer.

Have patience, O God, as I strive to be a person of prayer.

—Mary Zimmer

My Thoughts & Feelings

There is a soul inside each one of us that is affected by all our roles but that is a unique creation of God. It is the part of ourselves created for communion with God alone.

My Prayer Journey

For this child I prayed; and the LORD hath given me my petition.

—1 Samuel 1:27 KJV

Baby's Growth & Development

Weight _____

Length _____

New Skills _____

_____

_____

Observations:

Memorable Moments

Twelfth Month

BABY AT

TWELVE MONTHS

*S*ometimes we hear parents and grandparents say, "But she's growing up so fast. I wish she could stay little for just a while longer." But that is a wish against all the physical, mental, and emotional impulses of any child.

Children's growth and development occur by change. Sometimes it seems gradual, and suddenly we notice a new skill. Often as mothers we just get comfortable with one "stage" of development when our child is on to the next challenge of growing up. And it is the child's changing that brings about our growth and development as mothers. We live in response to their changing needs and demands, letting go of our control over who they are going to be just a little bit more each time.

The same model applies to our own growth in faith. The faith we had as adolescents expands with spiritual experience as we grow and change. For some, this kind of change is the hardest to bear. But our changing perceptions of God do not mean God actually changes. We don't have that kind of power.

The model of Christian growth described in the New Testament is one of growing up into Christ, facing new challenges to our faith and beliefs. Faith that does not grow becomes stagnant.

O God, may I always continue to grow up in Christ.

—Mary Zimmer

My Thoughts & Feelings

Children lead us to an even deeper understanding of God's gift of life.

My Prayer Journey

All your children shall be taught by the LORD, and great shall be the prosperity of your children. —Isaiah 54:13 NRSV

125

Baby's Growth & Development

Weight _____

Length _____

New Skills _____

_____

_____

Observations:

Memorable Moments